PAINTING OF THE WESTERN WORLD

IMPRESSIONISM

PAINTING OF THE WESTERN WORLD

IMPRESSIONISM

by Ian Barras Hill

Galley Press

Library of Congress Catalog Card No.
79-5366
ISBN 0-8317 4887 7
Manufactured in the Netherlands

Contents

Color illustrations

CHAPTER I

The Nineteenth Century Background to Events

Light years ahead – The anti-classical movement – The New Realism; Corot, Millet and the Barbizon School – Classicism v Rusticism.

The appeal of the landscapes and portraits of the Impressionists to modern eyes can be summed up in one word: – optimism. In no other art does the sheer vibrating colour and joy of living come over so strongly. We think of the blooming peach-skinned voluptuous nudes of Renoir; or the shimmering opalescent sun-kissed scenes of Monet painted at Argenteuil or Antibes; or the rousing carefree café-concert society so lovingly captured by Degas and Toulouse-Lautrec. Every Impressionist painting has an energy about it as though it's keeping beat with the rhythm of life. It throbs, glows, radiates and pins down, if only for a fleeting moment, the atmospheric and poetic truth of any given scene. It is to the boundless enthusiasm and optimism of Impressionist works that we respond so wholeheartedly even a century after they were painted. It was with their first group show in Paris in 1874 that the great names of Monet, Renoir, Degas, Sisley and Pissarro became known to the French public. They brought about a revolution in artistic approach and technique by painting out in the open air and loudly proclaiming the supremacy of light, not form or content, as the sole guiding principle in their work.

By the middle of the 19th century in France, the old classical values that had held for so long as a legacy from Renaissance and Baroque art were being seriously questioned. Foremost amongst these was the idea that beauty was only found by copying antiquity. No longer was there widespread patronage. The new spirit of rationalism and scientific enquiry pervaded every sphere of life. The books that were being read at the time were Darwin's *The Origin of Species* (1859) and later Marx's *Das Kapital*.

The result was a turning away from all things classical. After the French Revolution, whose events had been so idealistically depicted by David and other French Salon neo-classicists, the force of realism with its scrupulous attention to ordinary local detail asserted itself in the works of Courbet, Daumier and Millet, the first generations of the 19th century. The paintings exhibited in the national institutions such as the Royal Academy and the Paris Salon were still dominated by doughty, mythological and historical works which dutifully won medals year after year. However, the original impulse behind this kind of art – imperial and militaristic celebrations – had been exhausted and the grandiose music

Jean-Baptiste Camille Corot
the founding father of Impressionism
Paris, Bibliothèque Nationale

that used to be played so loud in praise of Napoleonic conquests now had a hollow ring to it. Instead of ranging far and wide over foreign lands in the unceasing quest for further territory, France now wanted to secure domestic peace and look inwards for political and spiritual nourishment.

Europe, with its resources exhausted and depleted, looked to its art and religion to lead the way. In France it was painters such as Corot, Millet and the Barbizon School who moved out of the war-ravaged and overpopulated cities to explore the countryside and live within an agricultural peasant community. Here they hoped to revitalise the sources of their art by observing the toil-worn, simple, labouring classes going about their grinding daily routine. The country folk's stoicism and long suffering was to be depicted as a symbol of national strength – the core and essence of the French character. Landscape painting started to assume a new importance and the Impressionists not only set about exploring the potential of this subject with a revolutionary zeal, but they also smashed many of the attitudes that had previously attached themselves to landscape painting.

One of these attitudes was that all art should have a strong narrative content; Monet and Degas rid their pictures of any literary meaning. Another was that landscape should be artificially arranged, bringing in hills from here and lakes from there to give a supposed harmonious balance, as in Claude's pictures. The Impressionists rejected all this. They were interested in how nature actually looked not what it was supposed to look like. In paintings such as Monet's *The Seine at Bougival* (1869) or Sisley's *The Flooding at Port-Marly* (1876) the interest is focused entirely on how shape and colour are affected by the play of light and atmosphere. All elements of the picturesque have been banished from the scene. It is as though we have picked up a snapshot and glimpsed a place exactly how it looked at that moment.

The Impressionists were amongst the first artists to break with the Renaissance tradition of perspective by deliberately constructing asymetrical scenes in order to focus more precisely on people or objects that fascinated them. Many of Degas's portraits of ballet dancers and singers were seen from eccentric viewpoints in order to emphasise a gesture or particular limb movement.

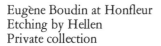

Eugène Boudin at Honfleur
Etching by Hellen
Private collection

8

CHAPTER II

The March of Industrialization

*The rebuilding of Paris - The Salon des Refusés (1863) -
The first Impressionist Exhibition 1874 - Edouard Manet
(1832-1883) - "Le Déjeuner sur l'Herbe" and "Olympia" -
Émile Zola and the Café Guerbois - The theory of Impressionism.*

Before we start our story, it is important to know about the background to all this change, for the mid-19th century in France was
an era of great change itself. Within two decades of the Second
Empire the merchant middle class was becoming an industrial
bourgeoisie. Important banks like the Crédit Lyonnais and Société
Générale were founded, in 1863 and 1864 respectively. The apogée
of Empire achievements was seen in the rise of Paris as a capital of
luxury and fashion with new department stores, newspapers, the
telegraph, the building of metal ships, all celebrated by the Uni-
versal Exhibitions in 1867 and 1889, and then crowned by the
building of the Eiffel Tower. However, this accelerating
industrialization upset the social order. Uprooted people flooded
into the towns, and a new working proletariat was born. In the
Paris of Balzac, all classes were mixed in the melting pot of the
main central areas. Napoleon III's architect, Baron Georges
Haussman sought to change this situation by driving the working
classes out to the far ends of the new thoroughfares he was
building in the centre of Paris.

The balance between city and country was torn apart. Industrial
society, the appalling drudgery of the mining communities, as described in Zola's novel *Germinal*, created proletarian masses who
stormed the barricades. In 1870 France was thrown into another
upheaval: the Franco–Prussian War, followed by the Siege of Paris
in which 36,000 people died of famine. Then came the Commune
uprisings during which 30,000 people were executed. "One of the
meanings of the Commune" wrote Henri Lefèbvre, "was the
return in force towards the urban centres of these workers driven
in the direction of the suburbs and the outskirts."

The new captains of industry, amassing fortunes as a result of
technical progress, wanted cultural symbols denoting continuity
and stability. They admired the polish and finish of a painting as
much as its content and their tastes were guided by the painter
Ingres who, as President of the École des Beaux-Arts, was the man
who most influenced aesthetic thinking in the first half of the century and pronounced:

"Classical figures are beautiful only because they resemble beautiful
nature. Any part of nature will always be beautiful when it resem-
bles beautiful ancient figures". Yet Ingres was a paradoxical personality. He was revered by Degas, Seurat and later Picasso for his

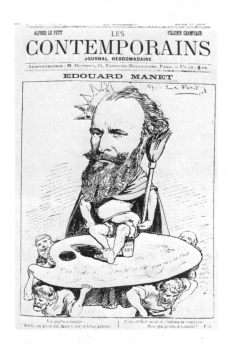

Edouard Manet
caricature by Alfred Le Petit
Paris, Bibliothèque Nationale

harmonies of tone, colour and geometry, but his practice was not as his preaching.

When Monet, Renoir, Sisley and Bazille were students in Gleyre's studio in Paris, they were pressed to study antiquity – Greek busts and bas-reliefs. "Let's get out of here, the place is unhealthy', said Monet, "there is no sincerity". All official art seemed to them like a wax mask which once removed revealed a lack of spiritual content. It fed too much on the past. It lacked spiritual élan.

It was largely due to the active support of the art dealer, Paul Durand-Ruel that the Impressionists received any sort of showing for their first paintings. He organised ten exhibitions of their work in London between 1870 and 1875, staged in his own private gallery. However, the public galleries in London and Paris were not so enthusiastic, and both Monet's and Pissarro's work was rejected by the Royal Academy. And back in Paris the group had to devise a plan of action to exhibit outside the Paris Salon and arrange their own show. The first blow against the establishment was struck on the 15th April 1874 when the First Impressionist Group Exhibition was held at the studio of the photographer Nadar on the corner of the Boulevard des Capucines, and was given the unwieldy title of "Société Anonyme des Artistes, Peintres, Gravures etc." Eight out of thirty exhibitors banded together to show solidarity of approach. They were Monet, Renoir, Pissarro, Cézanne, Degas, Sisley, Boudin and a lone woman Berthe Morisot, a friend of Manet's and a former Salon exhibitor. One of the paintings on view was destined to give the exhibition a name which would stick. It was called *Impression: Sunrise* by Monet, and upon seeing it the critic, Louis Leroy of the satirical magazine "Le Charivari" coined the word "Impressionism", and hurled it as a term of abuse at the group. One cartoon of the occasion showed a policeman preventing a pregnant woman from entering the exhibition for fear of injuring her unborn child.

These "slap dash" paintings flew in the face of all conventional expectations. The French Salon was enraged. Up till then no painter could successfully hope to make a respectable reputation for himself unless he won the approval of the Salon which, since the 17th century had enjoyed a prestige unrivalled in Europe. Its galleries were full of dutiful, neo-classic mythological and historical paintings. They were thoroughfares where crowds could come and go, stopping to note the prices of pictures, then stroll, gossip and take refreshment. In the Impressionist's time, the walls were crammed full of pictures by men like Jean-Léon Gérôme who dubbed the new men's work as "filth"; Bougereau, known as "The Raphael of the Bon-Marché", (a popular department store in Paris) whose paintings were the apotheosis of cloying good taste in their depiction of candy floss nudes; Meissonier, a finicky battle-scene painter and Alexandre Cabanel famous in his time for the *Birth of Venus*, a voluptuous riot of pink and white marbled skinned nudes, perhaps the epitome of meretricious sugar-sweet voyeurism. The latter painting was bought by Napoleon III from the Salon in 1863, that seminal year for modern art in which the Salon des Refusés was held.

In the spring of that year 5,000 paintings were submitted to this temple of art, the Salon des Beaux-Arts, of which 3,000 were rejected by the jury. The Administration wished to stem the tide of work by new artists which they believed might become "un danger sérieux pour la société". Louis Napoleon decided to find out what all the fuss was about and paid a surprise visit to the Salon. He considered some of the paintings to be quite good and ordered that all the rejected works be hung in the adjoining Palais d'Industrie, which became known as the Salon des Refusés. Pissarro, Cézanne and the American, Whistler all sent in work but it was a submission of Manet's *Le Déjeuner sur l'Herbe* (Luncheon on the Grass) that proved to be the "cause célèbre", a crowd-puller and a show stopper. What the public came to see was a painting of two young men, dressed, and two young women, one partially dressed and the other stark naked, picnicking in a wooded glade. The nude girl gazes out of the picture with an unaffected look of such charming insouciance that the sheer nerve and cheek of it scandalized the critics. The huffing and puffing must have been a sight to behold. "A commonplace woman of the demi-monde, as naked as can be, shamelessly lolls between two dandies dressed to the teeth" a critic remarked and went on to say that "this is a young man's practical joke, a shameful open sore not worth exhibiting this way".

When the Emperor and Empress paid a visit to the Salon, they were outraged by the picture. After examining it, the Emperor said, "Ce tableau offense le pudeur." The Empress pretended it wasn't there. The Beaux-Arts academicians replied: "We warned you, Sir, and this is the result" and went on to say that the work was just one amongst many by a bunch of dangerous subversives. The Emperor ordered that the Salon des Refusés never be repeated.

To a public led to expect stories from pictures, *Le Déjeuner sur l'Herbe* was a baffler. Manet himself was genuinely bewildered and hurt by the reaction. The painting, although freely adapted, contained classical references to Giorgione's *Fête Champêtre* in the Louvre and was a serious reworking of another artist's composition, a common practice whereby artists can identify and cross refer their methods with other great works, of the past. Velasquez, Manet's great hero, copied many of Titian's works for practice, whilst Van Dyck, the great Flemish portraitist who was the star pupil of Rubens' workshop from 1617 to 1621, borrowed compositional ideas from his master in his religious paintings. In this century the Velasquez portrait of Pope Innocent X inspired Francis Bacon's series of screaming Popes, and Picasso happily reworked compositions by Titian and Ingres to suit his ever-changing stylistic idioms. *Le Déjeuner sur l'Herbe*, far from being a visual cock-snook at European traditional sources, as its detractors claimed, was in fact on an Italian Renaissance engraving by Marcantonio Raimondi after Raphael.

The elegant, dandified Manet was no rampant revolutionary foaming at the mouth from the checks and reverses heaped upon him by polite society. He came, like Degas, from a solid upper

Edouard Manet
drawing by Edgar Degas
Private collection

11

— A la bonne heure, comtesse, on n'est pas plus spirituel-
lement impressionniste !
— Mes comp'iments, messieurs, toujours impressionnables!

JURY DE PEINTURE

— Vous reconnaissez avoir commis ce tableau? Avez-vous
des complices? Faites-vous partie de la bande de M. Manet?

middle class background and at the time of *Le Déjeuner sur l'Herbe*, had already been accepted in polite artistic society. Indeed two years previously a portrait of his parents and *The Guitarist* had been accepted by the Salon and, as the momentum for the Impressionist cause got going, his work continued to be accepted by the institutions, a fact which set him apart from the others who were fighting a battle on another front.

Although labelled as the leader of the Impressionist movement, he was far more akin to Degas who repeatedly denied that he was an Impressionist at all. Before Manet was hailed as the crusading champion of Impressionism it was the battle-scarred Gustave Courbet, the arch realist and scourge of middle-class propriety, an avuncular, belligerent Romantic who carried forth the banner of hopeful renewal in subject matter and approach. Almost twenty years their senior, Courbet was fast fading into cosy middle age, and it was to Manet that the younger men now looked. Manet, Renoir, Sisley *et al* became known as "La Bande à Manet" – Manet's gang.

Even before allowing the shockwaves generated by his picture at the Salon des Refusés to fully subside, Manet was putting the finishing touches to another painting that was destined to have the same explosive effect on traditional sensibilities and attract the same notoriety as *Le Déjeuner sur l'Herbe*.

This was a portrait of a young woman lying on a bed, naked, with her left hand gently resting on her "mons veneris", and wearing only a bracelet, earrings and a neck choker.

Again, as with *Le Déjeuner*, it was a painting based on another picture, this time it was Titian's *Venus of Urbino*. And again the look of the woman as she gazes unconcernedly out of the picture, with no hint of modesty or decorum, reminds us of the same device used in *Le Déjeuner* – an attempt to engage our interest and senses by the bold challenging promise of sexual mystery and pleasure. Manet called it *Olympia* in an open acknowledgement of its classical antecedents.

The Salon accepted the picture in 1865, but again a Manet work sent shockwaves through the whole establishment. It was a plain, unglamorous treatment of the female body, unmatched for candour since the nudes of Cranach nearly four centuries earlier. One critic asked: "What is this Odalisque with a yellow stomach, a base model picked up I know not where, who represents Olympia? A courtesan, no doubt". Baudelaire, the poet, a close friend of Manet's saw in her "a fusion of candour and wantonness... her arms, her legs, her thighs and her loins glistening as if polished with oil".

Here was another smack in the eye for the critics and many of them recoiled at the corpse-like treatment of the flesh. Goutier called it "a puny model stretched out on a sheet... the colour of the flesh is dirty, the modelling non-existent. The shadows are indicated by more or less large smears of blacking. What is to be said of the negress... or of the black cat which leaves its ugly footprints on the bed?" Courbet remarked: "It's flat, it isn't modelled; like the Queen of Spades on a playing card just out of her bath."

12

Edouard Manet
photographed by Nadar
Paris, collection Sirot

Olympia drew even greater crowds than *Le Déjeuner*. It was the only picture the public wanted to see. They thronged twenty foot deep around it, and had to be physically kept at bay by a pair of burly guards.

With these revolutionary paintings, Manet sent up two flares to announce the arrival of modern art. For this he was attacked from all sides and angrily berated by the critics. The influential ones, however, the novelist Zola, Victor Hugo and Baudelaire leapt to his defence. Zola had met Manet in February 1866 and set about championing the Impressionist cause with a zealous fervour through the popular press. In *L'Oeuvre* (1886) one of the twenty novels that make up "the natural and social history of the Rougon-Macquart family", Zola's great saga series, he tells the story of Claude Lantier, a painter and Pierre Sandoz, a novelist; a story clearly based on the struggles, successes and failures in the literary and artistic world of Paris which Manet, thinly disguised as Lantier and Zola, as Sandoz, experienced. The character of Lantier is an amalgam of Manet and Cézanne. Zola said: "With Claude Lantier I want to depict the struggle of the artist with nature, the effort of creation in a work of art, the blood and tears involved in giving one's flesh to create something living, the perpetual battling with truth, the endless failures, the ceaseless wrestling with the Angel." Passion in friendship, passion in love and passion in work is the picture Zola paints of Lantier's "gang", earnestly debating the issues of the day at their favourite Café Guerbois in the Avenue de Clichy.

For the next ten years, Manet provided the tiny band with a stirring example of creative energy in motion. He turned out portraits, flower studies and days at the races. He would quickly respond to news events and rush to the scene to record them. He went out in a small boat on a summer's day in 1864 when the Union corvette Kearsage engaged the Confederate privateer Alabama in a gun battle off Cherbourg and he painted the conflict with all the speed of a press photographer. He alone of the Impressionists painted scenes of war. (Interestingly, the group's critics have often accused them of giving an unbalanced view of the world, neglecting the class struggle, the war, famine and industrial turbulence that raged around them.) Manet, however, faced the issues of the time. One famous painting shows the execution of the Emperor Maximilian, who had originally been helped by French troops to seize power in Mexico in 1867. Manet was so disgusted at this betrayal by Louis Napoleon, who had abandoned Maximilian to his fate under pressure from the United States that he dressed the firing squad in French uniforms and modelled the scene on Goya's masterpiece *The Third of May*.

Through all this Manet remained very much an individual, allying himself with the other Impressionists only in their espousal of the broad aims of the cause such as painting out of doors and catching the immediate truth of an impression with boldness and depth. Although absent from the first Impressionist exhibition in 1874, he went out painting on the Seine with Monet and Renoir. In the same year he travelled to Venice and painted the city in glowing colour using short, sharp dab strokes of primary colours. He soon returned though, to the twilight, demi-world of Parisian night life and began painting a stunning series of richly assorted subjects – bars, circuses and "cocottes" – until his death in 1883 at the age of fifty two.

The theory of Impressionism

The chief tenets of Impressionist thinking were:

1. Truth to sensation; the painter cannot be false to visual reality.
2. Light governs all; it suffuses all objects and drenches texture and material.
3. Shadows are complementary tones which receive their hues from surrounding primary colours. Black must never be used.
4. Paintings are fragmentary sections of nature, not idealised compositions contrived and balanced.
5. Exercises in perspective are not pursued as ends in themselves. Depth is made indistinct and hazy, and space is rendered in two dimensions.
6. By ringing the changes in the chromatic register, improvising and refining the colours in the spectrum, new variations of optical sensation reveal themselves and force the spectator to respond such bold interpenetration of matter and material.

All these points are seen nowhere better than in Monet's work. He carried optical experimentation furthest and developed the idea of treating the same motif from a variety of angles in different light and weather conditions. In 1877 Monet treated an undoubtedly novel subject which had totally transformed peoples' lives at the beginning of the century – the train. He executed a series of superb paintings inside the Gare St. Lazare and managed to convince the station master that he was a Salon celebrity. Renoir recalled: "the trains were halted; the platforms cleared; and the engines were crammed with coal so as to give all the smoke that Monet desired". The belching steam from the locomotives under the bridge was painted misty blue. In *Le Pont de L'Europe*, we can glimpse views of the Rue de Rome and Les Batignolles through the wreathing smoke. Here Monet seemed to be painting an ugly goods yard as if it were a Normandy landscape. There was no precedent to viewing the architecture of heavy industry as material fit for art. Monet set it.

Letter from Edouard Manet with caricature of Eva Gonzales and her new husband Henri Guérard after their marriage in 1880 Paris, Bibliothèque Nationale

CHAPTER III

Claude Monet (1840-1926)
The Founder of Impressionism

The formative years with Boudin in Normandy – Poverty and neglect – At peace in war; Monet and Pissarro in London during the Franco-Prussian War – Paul Durand-Ruel – Argenteuil 1874-1877 – The break-up of the group – At Vetheuil with Madame Hoschedé – The elements explode; the final paintings at Giverny.

In current jargon, the first important "contact meeting" to occur between the Impressionists came when Claude Monet, all set to become a commercial artist at the age of 18, met Eugène Boudin in Le Havre, in 1858. Boudin was born in Honfleur and had spent most of his childhood in Le Havre where his father had a bookshop. Legend has it that Boudin, a beach scene and harbour painter, after seeing some drawings of local views by the young Monet in the window of a stationer, asked the new artist to accompany him on painting trips around the coast. It was under Boudin's wing that Monet first came to perceive and enjoy the pleasures of painting out of doors and the subtleties of sunlight and water. Soon after, however, Monet's parents sent him to Paris where he enrolled at the Académie Suisse, an enlightened establishment on the Quai des Orfèvres and it was there that he first met Camille Pissarro. But France was not to hold him for long, as he was drafted into the army for national service and posted to Algeria. Two years spent there stimulated his senses: the heat, light and colour of the place saturated his will and soul; he was to return to France determined to introduce to his palette a whole new chromatic range of higher-keyed colours, and to commit himself to landscape painting. In 1862 he met up again with Boudin, who introduced him to the brilliant young Dutch painter, Jongkind, who was working with Boudin in Normandy. Jongkind's seascape and windmill scenes show a deft looseness and lightness of touch anchored firmly to a sure Dutch compositional base, and were much admired by the young Monet. It can be said that both Boudin and Jongkind were the true initiators of Impressionism. Once again in Paris in the same year, Monet made friends with Renoir, Sisley and Bazille and the four of them made regular excursions to Barbizon, a little hamlet on the fringe of the Fontainebleau Forest where they joined Corot and other members of the Barbizon School to paint landscape out-of-doors. His parents, resigned now to the fact that their son was determined to become a painter, intended that he should enter the École des Beaux-Arts; when he refused to enrol, they cut his allowance. To further complicate matters, he met a young girl, Camille

Claude Monet, 1880
brush and ink by Edouard Manet
Basle, private collection

Claude Monet's garden at Giverny
Japanese bridge

Doncieux, who became his model and mistress and shortly after became pregnant. Against a rising tide of debts, the stubborn Monet burned two hundred of his paintings rather than give his creditors the satisfaction of helping themselves to the few possessions he had. Both Monet and Pissarro suffered appalling financial and domestic difficulties in the 1860's and 70's. Monet spent the summer of 1866 in Ville d'Avray near St. Cloud, the little village where Corot lived, and set about painting a picture in the open. He dug a trench in his garden and lowered a huge canvas into it so that he could work on the upper half. His wife Camille posed for this picture which he called *Women in the Garden*. Once finished, he returned to Le Havre in the autumn of 1866 in order to escape his creditors. His friend, Frédéric Bazille helped to ease his financial burden by buying *Women in the Garden* for 2,500 francs but this was not enough and at one point he had to leave the pregnant Camille. When Boudin visited him in 1869 he found him "completely starved, his wings clipped" after the birth of their son, Jean, in July. It was only then that he married her, and took her to Trouville; there he painted some bright beach scenes, shortly before departing for England that summer when the war broke out. The family sailed for London for, unlike Degas and Bazille, Monet was determined to avoid the draft.

Once in London he joined Pissarro, who had also made the trip across, and they sought out the works of the two English painters whose dazzling landscapes had so impressed visitors to the Paris Salon of 1824 – Turner and Constable. By this time English artists

Mary Cassatt at her château de Beaufrère with the Durand-Ruel family

had made great advances in their new, light and airy approach to landscape; this same exhibition, forty-five years previously had shown a display of stunning virtuosity in watercolour work by the precociously talented Englishman, Richard Parkes Bonington, who spent most of the twenty-six years of his short life travelling through France, looking for subjects, the like of which was not to be seen until the first Impressionist exhibition in Paris. Of their London life, Pissarro, in later years, recalled that: "Monet worked in the parks, while I, living in Lower Norwood, studied the effect of fog, snow and springtime".

Perhaps the greatest break for these two impoverished painters was an introduction through the Barbizon painter, Daubigny, to the art dealer Paul Durand-Ruel who was one of those beneficent patrons in whom judgment and taste combined in equal measure, and who was prepared to pay good cash for works in which he had absolute faith but no immediate hope of financial return, let alone profit. He paid Monet and Pissarro two and three hundred francs each for their paintings, at least five times as much as they were getting elsewhere. Between 1870 and 1875 he organised ten exhibitions in London and showed paintings by Manet, Monet, Sisley, Pissarro, Renoir and Degas. For this he was widely criticised, but he went on buying Impressionist paintings although they made no money for him; when he returned to France he had lost so much that he had to stop buying. Fortunately he managed to restore his fortunes to such an extent that by 1880 he was buying Impressionist paintings again, although he was more than a million francs in debt. "I would like to be free to go away and live in a desert" he confessed to Pissarro.

In 1886 he organised the first Impressionist exhibition in New York, followed by a second the next year; at the same time he opened his own gallery there. Both exhibitions were successes and it was largely due to his steadfast support during the lean years that the painters who showed there all managed to sell their paintings and add to their growing reputations. Durand-Ruel at last came to reap the fruits of his labours, and became rich.

Just as Boudin had introduced Monet to the pleasures of painting out-of-doors, so Monet in his turn took Manet with him to Argenteuil and other spots along the Seine, like Le Bougival, in 1874. With the aid of a neighbour, Gustave Caillebotte, a man who later became an ardent collector of Impressionist pictures, Monet made himself a special studio-boat in which he glided up and down the Seine painting bank and field scenes from the river. Monet had a particularly hard year in 1875. Time and time again he had to beg friends to lend him money. He approached Manet, Zola and Cézanne's patron, Victor Chocquet. At one point it looked as though he would have to give up painting entirely for lack of funds. In the autumn of 1877, with his wife expecting a baby, he asked Chocquet to take canvasses from him at any price he would offer, forty or fifty francs. Manet visited him at this time and found him quite broken down and in despair. Manet took it upon himself to pay Monet 1,000 francs "against merchandise" on January 5th 1878 and this helped the painter settle his debts in

Claude Monet in his studio

Argenteuil and pay advance rent for a house in Vetheuil on the banks of the Seine, far away from Paris. But before Monet left the capital he had to appeal again to Dr. Gachet for money and then in April to Zola. "Can you help me? We haven't a single sou in the house, not even anything to keep the pot boiling today. On top of this my wife is ailing and needs care, for as you probably know, she has given birth to a superb boy. Could you lend me two or three louis, or even only one...?"

His bad luck continued. His longtime patron, Ernest Hoschedé went bankrupt. Ernest Hoschedé was the director of a Paris department store who was one of the first collectors of works by Pissarro, Sisley, Monet and Degas. At an auction sale of his collection in 1874 some of his pictures fetched fairly high prices and it was largely due to the success of this sale that the Impressionists felt confident enough to mount their first Group exhibition on April 15th, 1874. However, in the summer of 1878 fortunes were reversed in a second sale of Hoschedé's collection that had been built up since the first auction. This time the prices for Impressionist pictures sunk to rock-bottom and some Pissarro landscapes were changing hands for as little as seven or eight francs! During that summer of 1878, Mme. Hoschedé left her husband and went to look after the ailing Madame Monet at Vetheuil and took along with her her six children. Monet was now painting fields of poppies and views of the Seine but was reduced to having to pawn his possessions to make ends meet. Camille was dying and her end was painful and long drawn out. Monet even painted her on her deathbed noting the fleeting hues of blue, yellow and grey on her face as the pallor of death set in. At such an act he felt a slave to his compulsion to paint all the time and compared himself to an animal who turns a millstone. However, he spent the autumn and winter at Vetheuil and Mme. Hoschedé took care of his two sons and managed the house. In deepest winter, he would plant himself on the banks of the Seine, dig his easel into the ice and then wait patiently like a fisherman in order to catch the fleeting violets, blues and pink shadows of the ice floes as they drifted downstream.

The following decade of the 1880's saw the gradual break-up of the group as each member went their own way to paint in increasing isolation; Monet to Giverny, Renoir to Cagnes in the South of France; only Manet, Degas and Pissarro remained in Paris but saw less and less of each other. It was no longer like the old Café Guerbois days of the 1860's. What was regarded as the first major defection was the decision by Renoir to show his large portrait of *Madame Charpentier and her children* at the Salon of 1879. It was received with great praise and Monet soon followed his lead by submitting two canvasses to the jury in 1880. To Degas this was an unforgiveable betrayal of the group's rules. He had long been scornful, yet resigned to Manet's yearning for official prizes and bourgeois respectability but for Renoir and Monet as well to defect to the other side, as he saw it, was the final abandonment of the common aims of the group. He accused Monet of "frantic log-rolling" and would have nothing more to do with him.

Monet's handling of paint had begun to change in the 1880's. The small, speckled dab strokes of his early work had lengthened out into more sinuous wiry strokes. He was fascinated by the fleeting effects of light and shadow on surfaces. In 1894 he painted a series of variations of the west front of Rouen Cathedral seen at different times of the day under changing light conditions. The Gothic facade served as an ideal fixed "motif" upon which he could indulge his obsession with recording the ephermeral atmospheric effects of surfaces bathed in undulating light waves. The facade floats and evaporates as its solid form eludes us. Just as in his final large canvasses painted in his water-garden at Giverny, Monet surrounds the spectator with a hazy mist in which the waterlilies advance and recede and float in a limitless mist. Perspective and gravity are disregarded. It seems we have to travel very little distance indeed to reach the 20th century colour abstractions of Jackson Pollock and that master of resonating colour atmospherics, Mark Rothko. And it was only with this move to Giverny with his new wife, the widowed Mme. Hoschedé thirty years his junior, that he found a new lease of life. His final series of bridges and waterlilies at Giverny, which he started upon in his seventies, was the resounding climax to an artistic career which never stood still in its quest to pin down the intangible magic of the whole visual field. These last Giverny paintings in their startling invention and grandeur can only be compard with Turner's last oils which hover on the edge of abstraction. They were done in the 1890's and early 1900's.

Monet died at the age of eighty six, in 1926, and never gave up right to the end. Cézanne said of him, "Monet is only an eye. But what an eye."

Claude Monet
photographed by Nadar
Paris, collection Sirot

CHAPTER IV

Edgar Degas (1834-1917)

"No art was ever less spontaneous than mine. What I do is the result of reflection and study of the great masters; of inspiration, spontaneity, temperament, I know nothing."

Degas's dislike of open-air painting – Strange new perspectives; mirrors, doorways and orchestra pits – Theatre, cabaret and café-concert life – His use of photography – The ballerinas and the pastel nudes – His ascetic bachelor existence – The loneliness and failing sight in the last years.

1. Eugène Boudin
Lady in white on the beach at Trouville, 1869
Oil on Canvas, 31 x 47 cm
Le Havre, Musée des Beaux-Arts

A native of Honfleur, Boudin went up the coast to Le Havre and saw some sketches of the area by the young Monet. Eugène Boudin had a great influence on Monet in his early years; he first met him in 1858 and, on Monet's return from Paris in 1862, he accompanied him on painting trips along the Normandy coastline and emphasized to him the importance of treating atmospheric conditions according to the place, time and wind. His studies of groups of society figures trouping across the beaches at Trouville and Honfleur are delicately wrought miniatures of great feeling and charm. In this study, his bold impasto technique suggests well the dark louring clouds and raking crosswinds that drove his elegant holiday-makers in hasty procession across the beach.

2. John Constable
Study for the leaping horse, 1825
Oil on canvas, 136 x 180 cm
London, Victoria and Albert Museum

Monet and Pissarro came to know Turner and Constable's work in London in 1870 whilst they were living there as refugees from the Franco-Prussian war. English oils and watercolours shown at the Paris Salon of 1824 had already opened Europe's eyes to the fresh and exciting new possibilities in landscape. The problem that now faced artists was how to reconcile the spontaneity of an oilsketch with the correct degree of finish demanded by the critics and public of the day. As Constable's other sketches show, the shifting effects of climate on landscape are often captured best by the quick preparatory study. This is but one study for *The Leaping Horse* of which there are many available.

Undoubtedly the most talented, enigmatic and magisterial member of the group was Edgar Degas. He shared the same background as Manet coming from the upper middle class. His family were wealthy bankers and intended Degas to take up a legal career, but after a classical education, he resolved to become a painter and attended L'École des Beaux-Arts. He first met Manet in the Louvre in the 1860's, when they were both copying Old Masters, and they mutually expressed their detestation of the academic stuffiness of the Salon, even though, ironically, they both regularly exhibited there after 1865. Degas, like the other Impressionists, was more interested in the pulsating life around him in the streets than the grandiose narrative sermons of history that cluttered the Salon walls. He did not, however, care for the Impressionists' spectrum palette and loathed open air painting to the extent of delivering a diatribe against "plein-airistes". "You know what I think of people who work out in the open," he said to Ambroise Vollard, his dealer, "I would have a special brigade of gendarmes to keep an eye on artists who paint landscapes from nature. Oh, I don't mean to kill anyone; just a little dose of bird shot now and then as a warning."

Degas preferred the theatre, opera house, cafés and cabarets. He told Pissarro and the others, "You need a natural life, I, an artificial one". Although in private life he was staunchly conservative, in public he was the most imaginative in seeking out new and unusual themes for artistic treatment. He forces the viewer to look at scenes from the most eccentric viewpoints and surprising angles. We see, for instance, the trapeze artist, Miss Lola of the Fernando Circus hanging by her teeth from a rope attached to the ceiling. Degas zooms up at her at the culminating point of her act as if using a telephoto lens. Many of his paintings of ballerinas in rehearsal, women washing themselves and horses strutting at the beginning of a race are given enormous dramatic impact by the bold, unexpected designs. People seem to be left high and dry in some closed off diagonal at the corner of a picture, leaving great areas of open space. Heads and bodies are cut off as in cropped

3. William Turner
Sunrise: a castle on a bay, c. 1840
Oil on canvas, 90 x 120 cm
London, Tate Gallery

Five years before this picture was
painted in 1835, Turner heralded
Impressionism with his *Norham Castle,
Sunrise*. This work must have been
executed after he returned from his
last trip to Venice because the vapor-
ous dissolving atmospherics of sunrise
that obliterate the castle are reminiscent of the methods Turner used to
enwreathe the city of Venice with
dazzling multi-coloured mists, that
dissolve all solid forms around it.
Turner, in his attempt to picture the
grandeur and sublimity of dramatic
natural scenery, as in his *Falls of the
Rhine at Schaffhausen*, moves technique
into the twentieth century with his
cosmic exercises in colour abstraction.
Monet was also swept away on a tide
of lyric wonderment.
They had much in common, both
preferring to fade away the physically
confining now with the promise of an
eternal ever-present by concerning
themselves with the magic of sun-
drenched buildings and lagoons which
vibrate with colour and space and
throw off sparkling reflections in the
water.

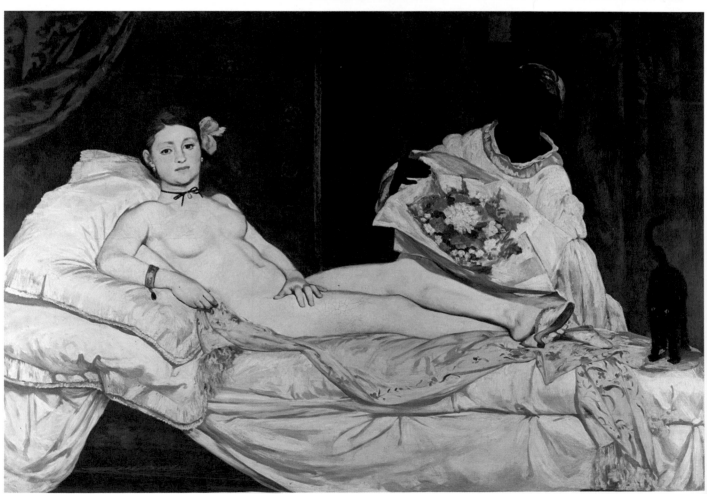

4. Edouard Manet
Luncheon on the grass, 1863
Oil on canvas, 208 x 264.5 cm
Paris, Musée National du Louvre

These two paintings on the left caused the most terrible outcry when they were shown in the Salon des Refusés on 1863 and the official Salon of 1865 respectively. Today, in this liberated age, one hardly bats an eyelid and it is hard to imagine the hysterical reactions with which these paintings were greeted in their time. *Le Déjeuner* was called indecent for showing two fully-dressed men in the company of a naked female bather. The utterly relaxed party consisted of Manet's favourite model, Victorine Meurend, his brother in law, the sculptor Ferdinand Leenhoff and Manet's younger brother, Eugène. The courageous defiance of these paintings made Manet a hero to the young painters who subsequently became the Impressionists. Monet was so impressed by the picture that in 1865 he painted his own version which shows, this time, a respectable clad party of picnickers assembled in a sunlit glade in the Fontainebleau forest. The painting is now in the Hermitage Museum, Leningrad.

5. Edouard Manet
Olympia, 1863
Oil on canvas, 130.5 x 190 cm
Paris, Musée National du Louvre

"What is this Odalisque with a yellow stomach, a base model picked up I know not where, who represents Olympia? Olympia? What Olympia? A courtesan no doubt" – so a critic scoffed, and such was the general tenor of abuse hurled at this work when it was shown in the Salon of 1865. Manet's intention in this famous painting was to bring the Old Master theme of reclining nudes à la Giorgione and Titian thoroughly up-to-date, but in the rapid fire of repeated attacks, his explanations somehow were silenced. The critics particularly objected to the way the paint had been used, for there was no attempt to disguise its existence as paint. Current Salon favourites, such as Bouguereau and Cabanel, used every sleek trick in their repertoire to simulate texture and disguise the surface.

6. Edouard Manet
Peonies, 1864-65
Oil on canvas, 91 x 69 cm
Paris, Musée National du Louvre

Most of the Impressionists at some time or another tackled flower and still-life painting but their reason for doing so was not to faithfully streak every petal like the 17th century Dutch artists; even less so to get bogged down in finicky detail. They sought to break up the structure and lay it in broad tones with directness and simplicity; to study the relationships of light and colour. This is what Manet does brilliantly in this vigorous study of Peonies. In a *Vase of Flowers* by Monet at the Courtauld Institute,

London, there is a marvellous vitality about the flowers and vase which merge in a sweep of flecked pink. The reflections of the dark blue of the vase are caught in the white table top emitting a coruscating shimmer found mainly in his seascapes.

7. Edouard Manet
Argenteuil, 1874
Oil on canvas, 149 x 131 cm
Tournai, Musée des Beaux-Arts

The golden years of Impressionism
lasted a decade, running from the late
1860's to about 1878. The unity of the
group was felt most when Monet,
Manet and Renoir painted landscapes
out-of-doors on the banks of the Seine
at Argenteuil. Monet spent the summer of this year at Gennevilliers
nearby. Renoir painted him at work
in his garden and Manet painted him
in his floating boat. Manet gained
sparkling effects by setting off light
accents against low tones and in this
study the lightness of the man's hat
and trousers and the furled sail awning
behind contrast dramatically with the
bright blue water. The Impressionists
were noted for their portrait studies
of informal naturalism of which this
is a fine example.

8. Claude Monet
Terrace at the seaside, Sainte Adresse,
1866
Oil on canvas, 78.8 x 129.5 cm
New York, Metropolitan Museum of
Art, Collection Rev. T. Pitcairn

The Rev. Theodore Pitcairn received
£588,000 for this Monet painting sold
at Christie's, London in 1976. He
bought the painting fifty years before
for less than £4,000. In April, 1979
another famous painting by Monet of
the railway bridge at Argenteuil, dated
1873, was sold at Sotheby's, London
for £420,000.

9. Edouard Manet
A bar at the Folies-Bergère, 1881-82
Oil on canvas, 96 x 130 cm
London, Courtauld Institute Galleries

Manet, like Degas, was fascinated by the glittering spectacle of the theatre and the café-concert. They both used mirrors to great effect to set up a number of radiating vantage points from which to survey all human activity. Here is captured the very essence of a hectic Parisian night spot. Manet was above all interested in spatial organisation. The bar maid placed in the middle with her short golden fringe and plaintive eyes is clearly not the only centre of attention. She is placed in juxtaposition to the other objects in the picture and is as much a still life as the bowl of oranges or the roses in the vase on the counter before her. Behind her we see a long-gloved lady peering through binoculars and gentlemen with stove-pipe hats. At the top left hand corner of the picture,

the legs of an acrobat cheekily peek down on a trapeze. All the bar details are lovingly described – the cluster of champagne bottles on the left is balanced by the Guinness bottle on the right. The picture was such a success at the Salon of 1882 that Manet was subsequently awarded the Legion of Honour, a prize he cherished.

11. Claude Monet
Rocks of Belle-Ile, or
The needles of Port-Coton, 1886
Oil on canvas, 65 x 81 cm
Moscow, Pushkin Museum of Art

Monet never tired of making trips up
and down the coast of Normandy
stopping at the most picturesque
spots. In 1882 he rented the Villa
Juliette at Pourville and made it his
base for visits to the surrounding
areas. He painted many rock outcrop
scenes, most memorably at Etretat
and Falaise, but here he treats the
rock structure just as he would a
country landscape, by blending in the
crashing white surf with the craggy
pinnacles. In such scenes, Monet
often decenters his landscapes by
leaving wide open areas of sea and sky
broken only by a grassy cliff top
which edges into the lower left
portion of the canvas.

10. Claude Monet
The magpie, 1867-70
Oil on canvas, 88.5 x 130.5 cm
Paris, private collection

Snow scenes offered the Impressionists the chance to highlight the
colours in shadows and show that
snow is not just white.

12. Claude Monet
The Houses of Parliament, London, 1903
Oil on canvas, 81 x 92 cm
Washington, National Gallery of Art
The Chester Dale Collection

On a return visit to London in later life, Monet became fascinated by the neo-Gothic architecture of the Houses of Parliament, and like Whistler, who was painting his *Nocturnes* at the same time, he drowned its silhouette in dense fog. He paints the river Thames as if it were the Grand Canal, Venice where water, sky and stone commingle. His method is well described by Gustave Geffroy who watched Monet at work beside the Thames. "He accumulated brushstrokes knowing exactly to which phenomena of light they corresponded. From time to time he would stop saying, 'The sun has gone down...' It was a grand sight, solemn and gloomy, an abyss from which a murmur came. One had the feeling that the atmosphere, everything was about to evaporate, disappear in a colourless obscurity: Suddenly Monet would seize his palette and brushes. 'The sun is out again', he said. At this moment he was the sole person aware of this."

13. Claude Monet
Rouen Cathedral-Albane tower at dawn, 1894
Oil on canvas, 104 x 74 cm
Boston, Museum of Fine Arts,
Tompkin Collection

Monet's series of pictures devoted to single subjects begins with the Gare Saint-Lazare, progresses through the Poplars and Haystacks and reaches its massive climax in the variations on the facade of Rouen Cathedral. The twenty canvases of this series of the cathedral seen at all times of the day were exhibited at the Galerie Durand-Ruel in 1895 and caused a sensation. Monet rented a room above a shop in Rouen, set up several easels before the window and spent long months there, studying the facade moving from one easel to another to catch the different nuances of colour at different times of the day. Georges Clemenceau, the statesman, said of them "we feel... the wave of an immense solar tide, rushing forward from infinite space, break in luminous waves, striking the stone with the entire light of the prism..."

14. Claude Monet
Water-garden at Giverny, 1904
Oil on canvas, 90 x 92 cm
Paris, Musée du Jeu de Paume

The last great works of Monet were a series of paintings of his water-garden and water-lilies at his house at Giverny. In 1890 he started to make improvements to the garden and formed a pond from a marshy tract, which he managed by diverting the course of the River Epte to make it flow through his garden. He had a foot-bridge decorated with wisteria built over the pond in the Japanese style and he planted exotic flowers, weeping willows, bamboo trees and rhododendrons. Ducks inhabited the lake. "My finest masterpiece is my garden" Monet said. He approached his subject with all the reverence of a man about to take communion. In his garden he had built a shrine for art. What he produced was far from deathlike, they are brilliant exercises in colour abstraction. – Water, plant and light coalescing into forms that tantalisingly hover. He attained this by softening the outline of plants and pond weeds, surrounding them with a misty haze.

The first series of Water-lilies comprised twenty-five canvases which were exhibited at the Galerie Durand-Ruel in 1900. Nine years later came a second series of forty-eight in which he left out the bridge and concentrated on the reflection of the water lilies, trees and vegetation on the banks and in the background. The light play of water and earth suggests the most amazing depths so that, mirror-like, we are transfixed by images that resonate all around us. "These landscapes of water and reflection have become an obsession" wrote Monet on August 11th, 1908.

15. Claude Monet
Regatta at Argenteuil, c. 1872
Oil on canvas, 48 x 73 cm
Paris, Musée National du Louvre

Monet had already celebrated the dancing play of light on water, the myriad reflections shifting with the ripples in his painting *La Grenouillère* on the banks of the Seine but he had yet to give his chromatic register full swell. Following his stay in London where he became acquainted with the works of Turner and Constable, he returned to Argenteuil to loosen up his technique and lighten his palette. Here he applies large brush strokes of divided tones to create vibrating colours that come together when viewed from a distance.

16. Pierre Auguste Renoir
Portrait of Claude Monet, 1872
Oil on canvas, 63 x 47.5 cm
Paris, Private collection

A sensitive study of the painter: a
calculated informality suggests that
the sitter is unaware of being painted
as he puffs his pipe and reads his
book.

17. Pierre Auguste Renoir
The luncheon of the boating party, 1881
Oil on canvas, 129.5 x 173 cm
Washington, The Phillips Collection

When Renoir painted this in 1881, he
had recently returned from Algiers
where the bright colours of North
Africa had lightened and intensified
his palette. It was painted at the
restaurant Fournaise on the island of
Chaton which is in the Seine on the
outskirts of Paris. The girl holding
the dog is Aline Charigot whom
Renoir was to marry in 1881. The
painter, Gustave Caillebotte, sits
opposite her with his back to the
viewer. The dappled rainbow-like
reflections that illuminate the scene
are typical of the warm sensuality that
Renoir brought to such pictures as *Le
Moulin de la Galette*.

18. Pierre Auguste Renoir
La Baigneuse au Griffon, 1870
Oil on canvas, 184 x 115 cm
Sao Paolo, Museu de Arte Moderna

We normally think of Renoir's nudes
as plump, blushing goddesses glowing
out at us from the canvas, solid,
sturdy limbed creatures. Renoir's debt
to his favourite 18th century painters,
Boucher and Fragonard, can clearly be
seen in this picture. Here he exercises
suitable restraint in his classical handling of the pose. "Such a girl needs
classic handling" Renoir was heard to
have remarked about this model. "The
Salon would have approved!"The
model was Renoir's young mistress,
Lise Tréhot, whom he painted in
another mythological scene as the
goddess, Diana in a style reminiscent
of Courbet, using a bold palette knife
technique.

19. Pierre Auguste Renoir
Mr. and Mrs. Sisley, 1868
Oil on canvas, 105 x 75 cm
Cologne, Wallraf-Richartz-Museum

Impressionist portraits are noted for
their easy naturalism and freshness of
colour. Here we see the newly
married Alfred Sisley and his wife.
Renoir makes the most of their
fashionable clothes to obtain a ringing
contrast between the red and gold of
Madame Sisley's dress and the dark
jacket of her husband.

20. Pierre Auguste Renoir
L'Estaque, 1882
Oil on canvas, 66 x 81 cm
Boston, Museum of Fine Arts

Both Renoir and Cézanne painted frequently at the little village of L'Estaque near Marseilles in the early 1880's and their approach to the same scenes show how their styles were rapidly changing at this time. In this picture we see the classic Impressionist treatment with sunshine and diffused light dominating the scene. Cézanne however, by this time had taken from Impressionism what he needed to build towards his geometrically structured landscapes. His *L'Estaque* of 1885 (Collection Lord Butler) shows how he applied the delicate colour gradations of the Impressionist palette to a more solid compositional substructure to give a force to his work that transferred the ephemerality of Impressionism into something more permanent.

21. Pierre Auguste Renoir
Portrait of Bazille in his studio, 1867
Oil on canvas, 106 x 74 cm
Paris, Musée National du Louvre

Jean Frédéric Bazille, born in 1841, came from the upper class of Montpellier society and there met the painter/patron Alfred Bruyas, a friend of his parents, who showed him the works of Corot, Delacroix, and Courbet. He came to Paris in 1861 to study medicine but abandoned this to devote himself to painting and entered the Gleyre studio in 1862 where he met Monet, Renoir and Sisley. He became particularly friendly with Renoir who was "so poor that he used to pick up empty paint tubes and still squeeze something out of them!" They both lodged together and thanks to Bazille's generosity, Renoir was able to work. Bazille also bought Monet's pictures when he was in dire straits. Every summer he would return to his family at

Montpellier and here painted his two most famous pictures – *The Family Reunion* and *View of a Village*, quiet works of classical composure in which the vibrant light of the Midi shone. When the Franco-Prussian War broke out in the summer of 1870 he enlisted in a light infantry regiment of Zouaves in Montpellier. He was killed in the Battle of Beaune-le-Rolande at the age of 29.
His work never really developed into Impressionism as it was too formally composed and photographic but it was in his handling of light and realistic treatment that he showed his kinship with the group.

22. Pierre Auguste Renoir
The bathers, 1887
Oil on canvas, 115.5 x 168 cm
Philadelphia, Museum of Art,
Collection Carroll S. Tyson

This is a late work of Renoir's, done
at a time when he had started to
renounce Impressionist doctrine to
introduce a harder more precise
modelling into his work. The theme
is taken from a sculptural relief at
Versailles by the 17th century sculptor
François Giradon. The painter's fantasy took flight here as he depicts the
girls sporting and frolicking like
nymphs in a Golden Arcady on the
Seine. The girl in the centre, so nicely
revealed, was his good friend and
model, Suzanne Valadon. It is
interesting to compare it with
Cézanne's treatment of the same
theme, so entirely different in
character.

23. Pierre Auguste Renoir
A girl with a watering can, 1876
Oil on canvas, 100.3 x 73 cm
Washington, National Gallery of Art,
The Chester Dale Collection

Renoir loved to paint children at play.
Here his method of suggesting
atmosphere and distance by merging
the subject of the foreground into the
same light as the background is well
demonstrated.
The red of the girl's hair ribbon and
the violet colour of her dress is
echoed by the flowers in the background. All outline is blurred with
the figure blending into a light-soaked
haze.

24. Camille Pissarro
Entrance to the village of Voisins, 1872
Oil on canvas, 45 x 55 cm
Paris, Musée de Jeu de Paume

Pissarro never veered from the broad
aims of Impressionism throughout his
life and strove always to recreate an
aspect of nature or piece of countryside faithfully so that the spectator felt
that he was actually there at the scene.
His advice to young painters was "Do
not define too closely the outlines of
things; it is the brushstroke of the
right value and colour which should
produce the drawing".

25. Camille Pissarro
Kitchen garden, trees in blossom, 1877
Oil on canvas, 65 x 82 cm
Paris, Musée National du Louvre

From 1872 to 1882, the middle-aged
Pissarro went to live at Pontoise, ten
miles north west of Paris in a rolling
countryside full of gardens and
orchards. He delighted in painting
many scenes of this area. He advised
others of his method: "Don't work
bit by bit but paint everything at once
by placing tones everywhere with
brushstrokes of the right colour and
value". Echoing Constable's words he
said; "One must be humble in front
of nature".

26. Camille Pissarro
Boulevard Montmartre in Paris, 1897
Oil on canvas, 73 x 92 cm
Leningrad, Hermitage Museum

Pissarro met the pointillists, Seurat and Signac, in the 1880's and became very excited about the new scientific methods of colour theory that they were expounding. He went to live at Eragny near Gisors and mingled in the market place there and at Rouen, sketching characters in watercolour and pastel. For the next two years his work shows a pointillist influence. After two successful exhibitions in 1890 and 1892 he started to travel again to Belgium, England, and various parts of France. But he was drawn like a magnet back to the metropolitan bustle and luxury of Paris and, like Manet, embarked, in his last years, on a series of city views – the Pont Neuf, the Tuilery Gardens and this grand panorama of the Boulevard Montmartre which he painted from a hotel window in 1897. The dense flow of traffic and pedestrians rushes up and down the street day and night in horsedrawn buses and carts mingling in a river of colour.

27. Camille Pissarro
Snow at Louveciennes, 1872
Oil on canvas, 55 x 46 cm
New York, Private Collection

Just look at the difference between
Sisley's treatment of a snow scene
(plate 30) and this one done by
Pissarro six years before. In the
Pissarro, the dark tree trunks make a
stark contrast against the snow and
further dramatic interest is obtained
by shuttering the shadows between
the trees making dynamic verticals
and diagonals as the sun fades at the
close of day. In the Sisley we see the
restrained uniform handling of tones
so characteristic of this painter. The
diagonal lines of the walls lead the eye
through the painting to the solitary
figure beyond, with the whole picture
held together by a pearly pink all-
pervading light.

28. Mary Cassatt
Young woman sewing, 1886
Oil on canvas, 92 x 65 cm
Paris, Musée National du Louvre

Mary Cassatt, like Berthe Morisot, the other leading female Impressionist, went through a classic art school education in Pennsylvania before coming to Europe in 1868. On arrival in Paris, she met Degas who greatly influenced her and they shared a love for Japanese prints. This accounts for the striking graphic qualities found in her art. Again, like Morisot, she had an affinity with young women and children. She adopted the pastel colouring and golden light of the Impressionists which she brought to her tenderly-felt portraits of young girls absorbed in some private pre-occupation.

29. Alfred Sisley
The banks of the Seine at Bougival, 1876
Oil on canvas, 38 x 55 cm
Private Collection

This is a subtle study in turquoise and greens, full of movement in the sky with its broken areas of cloud. It is tinged with Sisley's slightly melancholy harmony.

30. Alfred Sisley
Snow at Louveciennes, 1878
Oil on canvas, 61 x 50 cm
Paris, Musée du Jeu de Paume

See caption for double page Pissarro snow scene at the same place, (plate 27).

31. Alfred Sisley
The flood at Port-Marly, 1876
Oil on canvas, 50 x 61 cm
Rouen, Musée des Beaux-Arts

This is perhaps the most famous of Sisley's pictures and his masterpiece. There are many versions. One hangs in the Louvre and in it the turbulence of the sky matches the full swell of the river. Like Constable, Sisley had an intuitive feel for the atmospherics of climate. The subtle muted grey tones with tints of blue glimmering through the clouds owe something to Corot. The rectangular shape of the corner café is counterbalanced on the right of the picture by the vertical telegraph pole and trees, leaving the vast open space of the water and sky to merge in a pinky blue harmony.

32. Berthe Morisot
The cradle, 1873
Oil on canvas, 55 x 46 cm
Paris, Musée National du Louvre

33. Berthe Morisot
Edma, the artist's sister, and their mother,
1869-70
Oil on canvas, 100.5 x 82 cm
Washington D.C., National Gallery
of Art

Berthe Morisot, the great friend of
Manet, was supreme when it came to
portraits of domestic interiors, sitting
rooms with mother and daughter
sewing and reading as the clock on
the mantelpiece ticks away, wearing
out the long hours. In the year of this
portrait (left) her style had percepti-
bly changed and she came to use a
lighter palette to obtain a true equil-
ibrium of harmony and colour. The
portrait of her mother and sister,
done earlier, shows the influence of
Manet in its rich dark colours. Note
how the black of her mother's dress
cuts across the creamy white of her
sister's – a favourite device with
Manet.

34. Edgar Degas
The cotton market, New Orleans, 1873
Oil on canvas, 74 x 92 cm
Pau, Musée des Beaux-Arts

Degas went to America at the outbreak of the Franco-Prussian War and it was there he discovered photography. This group portrait, which shows his uncle's office in New Orleans with family members and staff, bears all the marks of a random press photograph with sharply cameos pieced together from individual snapshots. Degas was know to have used a camera to arrange the composition of his larger paintings, such as the *Bellelli Family* in the Jeu de Paume, Paris.

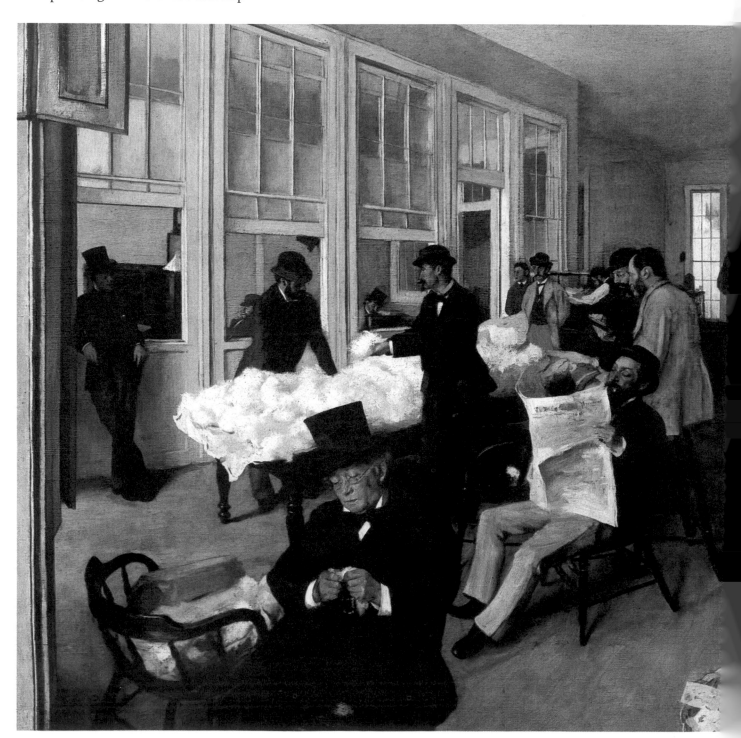

35. Edgar Degas
Musicians in the orchestra, 1872 (Opera
Orchestra)
Oil on canvas, 69 x 49 cm
Frankfurt, Städelsches Kunstinstitut

36. Edgar Degas
The dancing class, c. 1874
Oil on canvas, 85.5 x 75 cm
Paris, Musée du Jeu de Paume

Manet, Renoir and Degas were all
captivated by the theatre. They loved
to observe the skills and artifice of
performance. But Degas' special
preserve was ballet. He could catch in
a few decisive strokes the muscular
effort and contortions that the "small
female monkeys", as Goncourt called
the young dancers, went through.
(See also plate 35.)

37. Edgar Degas
After the bath, woman drying her neck,
1898
Pastel on cardboard, 62 x 65 cm
Paris, Musée du Jeu de Paume

The human figure was the centre of
Degas' work. But at the end of his life
it became an obsession. He adapted
the precious, elegant technique of
pastels best known from the portrait
studies of 18th century artists like
Fragonard, to chronicle the boudoir
activities of women. Women seen
washing, drying themselves and

combing their hair. "Painting is one's
private life", he said, and for Degas, a
bachelor with misogynist tendencies,
this became an all-consuming reality.
His cool, dispassionate eye caught the
most private moments of the shop
girls and seamstresses he hired as
models, and recorded them as if seen
through a keyhole. "It is the human
animal busy with herself" he told the
writer, George Moore, "a cat licking
herself".

38. Edgar Degas
Racehorses at Longchamp, 1873-75
Oil on canvas, 30 x 40 cm
Boston, Museum of Fine Arts

At the races at Longchamp, near Paris, Degas observed the horses and riders at close quarters. Not a betting man, he was uninterested in who won. His forte was to capture the tense preparations of a race meeting with the horses strutting and stamping before the starting line, and to mark the effects of the driving rain as it both blurred and gave a sense of speed, as in an out-of-focus photograph.

photographs. This, and the light he used to heighten all this drama, was all intentional. It won him the awed respect of the other Impressionists. He cuts faces in two with scything shafts of light; half the face glows in a spotlight whilst the other is obliterated in shadow. In *Le Café des Ambassadeurs* the eye is led straight up to the singer on the stage by her garish red dress. To the right, the shepherd's crook shape of a musician's double bass bites into the brightness of the dress, etching in a dynamic contrast. This was a device that Toulouse-Lautrec used to such effect in his Moulin Rouge posters.

Degas laboured long and hard to achieve these naturalistic effects. "When I die, they will see how hard I worked," he said. He was aided in his pursuits for new perspectives by the advent of photography, and only started to really explore the potentialities of the medium when he reached the United States in 1870, having sailed there at the beginning of the Franco-Prussian War. A work of this period *The Cotton Exchange* shows his uncle's office in New Orleans with figure portraits of family and staff. As a composition it seems as random and haphazard as a press photograph but as always with Degas, it was artfully contrived. On return to Paris he linked up again with his old friends – Manet, Renoir and Pissarro – but strictly on his own terms. A cautious, reserved man, he had little time for the bohemian argy-bargy and knock-about comradeship that make artistic groups the stuff of popular myth. Soon a series of financial mishaps within the family nearly reduced him to the straitened circumstances of his friends. He had to sell his substantial collection of pictures to help settle his brother's debts, and now became more dependent on selling his work to live. His answer was to make it more popular.

With this new situation, he threw himself into a frenzy of work. He loved to observe the rituals of training that all performers had to go through to polish and perfect their skills. Unerringly, he pins down the labour and strain of ballet rehearsals. Degas catches their weary, frail bodies in the half light of rehearsals, and homes in on those brief, unguarded moments just as they are adjusting their slippers, doing up their hair or simply relaxing in a crumpled heap on the floor. With Degas we are always aware of having stumbled across an extremely private scene; he frames cameos from unguarded moments. Yet even in his nude studies, he keeps his distance as the dispassionate observer. His women have none of the sensual warmth of Renoir's but lack nothing for that. If anything they are more fascinating. He liked to think of himself as simply an eye interested only on the colours, movements and materials of the girls. A girl glimpsed in an open door, the rakish angle of a hat, the set of a woman's body as she washes clothes or irons, these are the points Degas focused on to bring reality to a scene.

A remark of his, when asked about his pastel portraits of nudes, is revealing. "I show them deprived of their airs and affectations, reduced to the level of animals cleaning themselves," he said of his models, without intending to insult.

Degas was in his fifties when he switched from oils to pastels,

Edgar Degas

largely as a result of his failing eyesight. It seems he may have contracted conjunctivitis caused by a chill caught in his nights as a sentinel during the Siege of Paris. The change brought about a remarkable late flowering of talent and produced work by which he is probably now best remembered – his pastel nude studies. His obsession with the human figure always set both him and Manet apart from the other Impressionists and it reached new extremes when he embarked upon this series of women going about their ablutionary routines – getting in and out of baths, combing their hair, washing and massaging themselves. He wanted to portray his nudes as if he had watched them through a keyhole and inevitably such a remark, made in a Victorian age, invited charges of lascivious voyeurism from some quarters. This was never his intention. He told the Irish writer George Moore, that his nudes represented "the human beast occupied with herself, a cat licking herself". These beautiful glowing studies were exhibited at the eighth and last of the Impressionist exhibitions in 1886.

Degas was now completely taken up with conveying the blurred movement and rhythm of a scene. His late pastels were like explosions of colour. One of the techniques he used to increase the luminosity of the pastels was to spray boiling water over them. The dry pastel then clogged into a paste which he could work freely on with a brush to give the consistency of a wash that could be spread about the paper. He went regularly to the racetrack at Longchamp to study the horses. He was most interested, not in the race itself, but in the preparations for it: the nervous anticipation of the horses as they strutted and stamped in the enclosures, awaiting starting orders. Such pent-up energy is seen well in *The False Start*. The drama and excitement lay in the ability, or not, of these refined, sensitive creatures to rise to the occasion.

"The artist must live alone, and his private life must remain unknown", Degas insisted. Certainly as a person he was unlike the other Impressionists, most of whom were married and had children. He professed to dislike children, dogs and flowers and was opposed to almost all social reform. He was sarcastic, abrasive and wary of friendship. The person who was closest to him during his life was the American painter, Mary Cassatt, who understood his complex and withdrawn personality. She called him "a pessimist" and Manet told Berthe Morisot, "He's anything but natural. He is incapable of loving a woman", an impression one also forms from the gist of his own remark "There is love, and there is work, but we have only one heart."

Although referred to as "that terrible Monsieur Degas" he was at heart, a reserved yet compassionate man whose occasional blustering fits of temper were attempts to guard his own privacy. He lived a frugal, ascetic bachelor existence in lodgings in the Ninth Arrondissement near the Opera, and never married. His last years seem pitifully sad. In 1908 he stopped work altogether as his sight failed and he used to be seen from about 1912 onwards wandering about the streets of Paris wearing an Inverness cape and a bottle green bowler. When he died in 1917 he left behind him an estate worth thousands of dollars.

Mary Cassatt in 1913

CHAPTER V

Belle de Jour: The Art of Pierre Auguste Renoir (1841-1919)

"It isn't enough for a painter to be skilful; one should be able to see that he loves to caress his canvas."

The painter of china ware - On the banks of the Seine with Monet in 1874 - "The Moulin de la Galette" - The Charpentier family - Algeria and the Mediterranean light - the glowing sensuous nudes - At "Les Collettes" at Cagnes in the South of France.

Degas and Renoir were as unlike each other as chalk and cheese. Pierre Auguste Renoir filled the world with pictures of cheerful, buxom girls; fair skinned Dianas whom he idealised and depicted also as ruddily healthy goddesses. Degas, on the other hand would never flatter his sitters. "Art", he once said rather drily, "cannot be done with the intention of pleasing".

The antithesis of Renoir, Degas once replied to a lady who asked him why he always made women appear ugly," Because women *are* ugly!" However his pastels showed that he too could obtain the same soft caressing effects as Renoir, whose visions of ample girls in the full flush of youth and women ripening into maturity are world famous. They all possess a sturdy sensuousness worthy of Rubens, but more refined in execution.

"Renoir" said the writer Octave Mirabeau, "is perhaps the only painter who never produced a sad painting". He was born at the other end of the social scale to Degas and Manet, being the son of a tailor at Limoges, and came to Paris when he was four. Surprisingly his parents were not opposed to his wish to become a painter and he started out by painting flowers on chinaware for five sous a dozen. He aspired to become a porcelain painter at six francs a day but his employer went bankrupt after a mechanical process replaced the old hand-drawn methods. He made frequent trips to the Louvre where he admired the works of the 18th century masters, Watteau, Boucher and Fragonard and he used some of their decorative designs in his work. After lessons at Gleyre's studio and a stint at L'École des Beaux-Arts, he joined Monet, a fellow pupil, in trips down the Seine where they both set up their easels on the banks and painted at Le Bougival in the late 1860's. There was a favourite boating and bathing spot known as *La Grenouillère* (The frog pool) where young Parisians with parasols gathered and the two young men sat there, side by side in 1869, painting the same scenes.

They learnt from each other. Monet influenced Renoir in his treatment of distance by fragmenting solid form into a prismatic patch-

Pierre Auguste Renoir painting
outside his villa at Cagnes

work of irridescent light laid onto the canvas with short brushstrokes of unmixed colours. Renoir on his part, encouraged Monet
to fill his landscapes with people and then merge the two, blurring
distinctions.

There was a cheerful optimism and sturdy resilience about Renoir
that served him well throughout his life. He certainly had to draw
on them at times. Both Monet and Renoir were stung by the gibes
of the critics after the Impressionist exhibition of 1874 when their
hope for commercial success seemed to be fast becoming a pipe-
dream. Impoverished and isolated, they pooled the few resources
they had and rented a studio. Into this they brought a single stove
on which to cook their food, and hired a model. Huddled together, they warmed themselves before the stove and it was only
with the appearance of Renoir's *Moulin de la Galette* painted at this
time, in 1877, that the critics seemed to get a bit warmer too.
Hailed as a masterpiece the painting shows the dancing, dining
and drinking in one of Paris's main pleasure gardens. It is a noisy,

Renoir's villa "Les Collettes" at Cagnes

happy, sunny picture filled with love and laughter which brightened everyone up at the time.

Fortunately there were some who supported the rebels through good and bad times. In Renoir's case it was his own brother, Edmond, who was the managing editor of a newspaper *La Vie Moderne* owned by an enlightened publisher, Charpentier. Into his house Charpentier welcomed such literary celebrities as Zola, Maupassant and the Goncourt brothers. Renoir also became a frequent guest and painted his host's charming, elegant daughters. "The forests of Fontainebleau" wrote Edmond "were better than the four walls of a studio to Renoir. Atmosphere and surroundings had an enormous influence on him... When he painted the *Moulin de la Galette* he settled down to it for six months, wedded to this whole world which so enchanted him, and for which models in poses were not good enough. Immersing himself in this whirlpool of pleasure-seeking, he captured the hectic moment with dazzling vivacity".

Instead of exhibiting with the Impressionists in 1879 and 1881, Renoir travelled to Algeria first for six months, then to Guernsey and in 1881, to Italy with his young bride, Aline Charigat. The sights and great art of the Renaissance painters impressed him greatly and forced him to take another look at the methods he was using and the direction in which he was going. "I had come to the end of Impressionism and had arrived at a situation in which I did not know how to paint or draw", he confessed later.

The Mediterranean light flooded onto his palette. From now on he concentrated almost entirely on paying his special homage to the female form in a series of alluring, sensuous nudes which glorify and revere women. Never before had an artist brought out the silky glowing translucence of a woman's skin, so effectively – and caringly. And again, another point of difference with Degas. Renoir's backdrops and settings are often so artificial. From out of perpetual seasons of mists and mellow fruitfulness emerge dappled Venuses cast in classical poses.

From 1903 onwards, Renoir and his family travelled regularly to their villa "Les Collettes" at Cagnes in the South of France, where the cooler hues of the north gave way to the warm, red, full blooded colours of the Riviera coast. The move was prompted largely as a result of his growing arthritis which paralysed his hands but he continued painting with brushes strapped to his wrists. In 1912, seven years before his death, Paul Durand-Ruel visited him at his house at Cagnes and found him "in the same sad state, but with that astonishing forceful character which never left him. He can neither walk nor rise from his wheelchair. Two persons are required to carry him everywhere. What torture and with all that the same good disposition and the same happiness when he can paint".

CHAPTER VI

Camille Pissarro, 1830-1903
Paul Cézanne, 1839-1906
Alfred Sisley, 1839-1899
Berthe Morisot, 1841-1895

The golden years of Impressionism are those from 1872 and 1882. Although many of the painters professed its aims, only two practised them consistently. They were Monet and Pissarro. Older than the others and a former pupil of Corot, Pissarro was looked upon as the father figure of the group. Born in the Virgin Islands he came with his shopkeeper parents to Paris to study at L'École des Beaux-Arts and the Académie Suisse. Throughout the 1860's his work, gentle, lyrical landscapes, hardly controversial, was accepted at the Salon, but as he moved out from under the shadow of Corot and his style changed, he couldn't sell his pictures and a period of near-destitution followed. Reduced to such straitened circumstances he could barely support the woman he was living with, his mother's former maid, and feed his children. In 1870 the Prussian army were advancing into the French countryside and had reached the outskirts of Paris. There, at Louveciennes a regiment seized his house for use as an abattoir and laid his canvases down as duckboards in the muddy garden. By this time Pissarro had fled to London where he joined Monet and the two of them painted London scenes out-of-doors. When they returned to Paris they found that although a new Republic had been declared, things were much as before. Their old idols had been punished or had disappeared. In the Commune riots of 1871, Courbet had been sent to prison for his part in pushing down the Vendôme column. Bazille had been killed in

Camille Pissarro with his portable easel box in the garden of his house at Eragny

Alfred Sisley

Letter from Camille Pissarro to
Madame Manet
(Berthe Morisot)
Private collection

Eragny par Gisors (Eure)
25 Juin 1891

Chère Madame Manet—
Mon fils Lucien fixé
à Londres me prie de vous demander
si vous consentiriez, en principe,
à faire partie d'une Société qui
vient de se former à Londres ayant
pour but de faire des expositions de
gravures, pastels, dessins, croquis &c.
composé de vrais artistes ayant nos
tendances et nos idées, si vous le
consentez vous recevrez avant me
un programme avec plus de ren-
-seignements. — J'ai accepté d'en
être, je serais très heureux si nous
pouvions compter sur vous.

Recevez, chère Madame
Manet, mes Cordiales salutations
C. Pissarro.

the war and the Salon was as reactionary as ever. The confiscation of property and money had left the bourgeoisie with less ready cash with which to buy pictures.

Pissarro now took under his wing Paul Cézanne, a painter from Aix-en-Provence who had stunned everyone with two paintings in the first Impressionist exhibition of 1874; one of them was called *A Modern Olympia*, a direct reference to Manet's notorious "dirty nude" that had so shocked the Salon in 1865. Pissarro first opened Cézanne's eyes to the fact that colour could be more than merely descriptive in landscape. Colours could control form and by the way they were placed side by side could vibrate and effect each other. Short brushstrokes, criss-crossed in parallel diagonals, tonally exact, could suggest both rhythm and depth of field. Cézanne was most influenced by Pissarro from the years 1872 to 1877 when he was living at Auvers-sur-Oise. Later it was the underlying structure of landscape which was to become an obsession for Cézanne. He wanted to "marry the curves of women to the shoulders of hills" in an organic interpenetration of all matter. The steadfast Pissarro never wavered from the cause and was the only painter to exhibit at every one of the eight Impressionist exhibitions. He encouraged the younger artists especially Gauguin and Van Gogh and it was not until the end of his life that he was duly recognised and honoured. Although always thought of as a landscape painter, he made some fine drawings and lithographs commenting on the social and political life of Paris.

Another landscape painter, although of lesser stature, was Alfred Sisley an Englishman born in Paris in 1839 and brought up there until he was eighteen. He studied briefly for a few months at Gleyre's studio before going out to Fontainebleau and St. Cloud. His early style was Corot-esque but he showed none of the innovatory skill that characterised Monet and Renoir's early work. When his father's business failed after the Franco-Prussian war he had to paint professionally for a living and it was at this point that he made notable advances in technique.
He excelled in depicting climatic effects of snow, gales, mists and floods and always captured the exact mood of a fleeting moment with subtle lyricism. He struggled under conditions of extreme poverty at times hardly managing to support his family and were it not for the loyal support of Durand-Ruel, Sisley might well have gone under. From 1885 he became more influenced by Monet and brought a flickering, glittering touch to his canvases which often has the effect of completely breaking down and dissolving the solidity of the composition.
After the death of his father in 1870 and his loss of a permanent income, he detached himself from the group to retreat to the solitude of Louveciennes and Moret. Monet came to his rescue in January 1899 when a sick and exhausted Sisley asked him to look after his wife and children only a week before he died. Sisley left a stock of unsold paintings in his studio and Monet helped to arrange a sale at Sisley's home at Moret-sur-Loing near

Berthe Morisot in 1875

Fontainebleau. As so often happens with artists, death brought its financial rewards. The tide had turned and the auction was a sell-out.

There is a limpid delicacy about many of Sisley's paintings which are tinged with melancholy and have a quiet appeal. He never strove for grand effects and worked on a relatively small scale. Because of this he was always considered to be a minor Impressionist, certainly he was not of the calibre of Monet or Degas, but size should never be the arbiter of worth. He and Pissarro between them painted perhaps the most restful and pleasing of all the Impressionist landscapes, and the ones that are the most familiar and best loved today. Apart from the support of his colleagues, Sisley received almost no recognition in his lifetime.

Berthe Morisot was a beautiful, refined and intelligent young woman who first was brought into the Impressionist circle through her friendship with Manet. She had great natural ability and, as the great-granddaughter of Fragonard advanced effortlessly through the upper reaches of Salon society. She exhibited at the Salon first in 1864 when she was twenty-three and had pictures accepted there without a break for the next nine years. She studied first with Corot but as she drew closer to Manet she started to respond to and admire the crusading zeal of the others. Against Manet's wishes she helped organise the first Impressionist exhibition in 1874 in which she showed nine works.

Like a lamb led to the slaughter, she attracted down on herself the scorn and abuse of the critics. One critic wrote after the second Impressionist exhibition in 1876:

"The innocent pedestrian attracted by the flags outside goes in for a look. But what a cruel spectacle meets his frightened eyes! Five or six lunatics – one of them a woman – make up a group of poor wretches who have succumbed to the madness of ambition and dared to put on an exhibition of their work... There is a woman in the group, as in all well known gangs. Her name is Berthe Morisot, and she is a curiosity. She manages to convey a certain feminine grace despite her outbursts of delirium."

The men were furious at these insults to her, but Berthe turned a blind eye. "She just laughed" Renoir recalled later.

Manet was first attracted to Berthe when he came across her copying a Rubens in the Louvre, and Fantin-Latour introduced them. He asked her to pose for him for the picture *The balcony* which appeared in the Salon the following year. Although strongly attracted to each other, it seems Manet kept his distance and there is no evidence to show that she ever became his mistress. Berthe might have liked to have lured Manet away from his comfortable, matronly wife, Suzanne, and married him but it was not to be. They continued their intimate friendship for six years until Berthe felt the years slipping away. Consanguinity was the answer and Berthe married Manet's younger brother, Eugène. They set up home in the Rue de Villejust which became a favourite meeting place of the Impressionists and a friendly haven for many of the young poets and musicians of the time.

CHAPTER VII

The Turning Point

Other European and American Impressionists – Georges Seurat (1859-1891) and Pointillism.

Impressionist methods were never strictly conceived of in terms of theory. They were mostly transmitted by word of mouth. However in the 1880's an attempt was made to provide a theoretic base, and this was explained and demonstrated in the work of Seurat, Signac and their followers. Recent scientific enquiries into the laws of optics by the French chemist, Chevreul, led Seurat to believe that it was now possible to formalise colour experimentation and objectively manipulate its effects by a rigorously methodical approach to paint application. The spectrum or the chromatic circle was now the bible. By re-assembling its constituent parts, the free techniques and loose empirical combinations of colour that Monet had taken to such an extreme could now be systemised.

This was done by juxtaposing small dots of colour – red, blue, violet, orange and green – in continuous relation to each other, using white to break the colours up for gradated tonal effect so that the whole lot fuse together, as in a mosaic, when viewed from a distance.

Seurat called his method "Divisionism" although it became more popularly known as "Pointillism".

It was Pissarro, always the most curious of the group, who was most enthusiastic about this new discovery and saw it as a way ahead for the Impressionists. Felix Fénéon, the propagandist of the movement, was quick to enlist Pissarro's support in order to win round the other Impressionists, but it was not to be. Both Monet and Renoir were still valiantly slaving away in the open air. To Monet now the whole world was awash in a sea of colour. For Renoir, nubile maidens and children had become an obsession. They looked on with bemused interest, mindful of their own early struggles, yet sceptical.

Seurat patrolled that same reach of the Seine that Monet and Renoir had already made their own. Its face though had changed. The marks of industry were everywhere. His *Sunday Afternoon on the Île de la Grande-Jatte* (1883-1885) imposes geometric order on a scene that shows women and children enjoying the sun and gently promenading in a public park. The glancing, stippled light effects convey well the sedentary after-lunch drowsiness that drenches and permeates his monumental *Une Baignade* painted when he was only twenty-four, and showing sun and river bathers idly strung along a bank of the Seine. The landscape behind shows the bridge at Courbevoie and the smoking factory chimneys of the industrial Paris suburb of Asnières, only four kilometers from Argenteuil.

Félix Fénéon, detail of a painting by Paul Signac New York, private collection

Boulogne Sands, 1892
painting by Philip Wilson Steer
London, Tate Gallery

He composed the picture in his studio from a number of small oil sketches which are completely Impressionist in character. It is the key transitional painting of the period.

The real change that Pointillism brought about was to shift the emphasis from the Impressionist ideal of capturing the illusory charm of the surface to the new possibilities of bringing out the intensity of primary colours in dazzling combinations that would outshine all that had gone before. It was to have a great influence on Van Gogh and the Expressionists.

Impressionism was not confined to France alone. Its influence spread to Europe and the U.S.A. A frequent traveller to Paris was the German Max Liebermann who studied with Manet and produced some fine pictures. Another Manet pupil, John Singer Sargent combined Old Master compositional poses with Impressionist techniques, to become England's leading portrait painter of the late 19th century. The most outstanding disciple was Walter Sickert, who lived and worked with the group in Paris and Dieppe and whose drawings and paintings of old London music halls, like the Old Bedford done in the 1890's showed a clear debt to Degas.

Philip Wilson Steer was the other notable English adherent whose beach scenes with girls playing at Walberswick, Suffolk are England's ethnic equivalent of Argenteuil-sur-Seine. In the U.S.A. Everett Shinn and Childe Hassam worked in the Impressionist vein.

CHAPTER VIII

The Lessons of Impressionism: the second generation

Sunshine and bright colour - Freedom of composition - The influence of Japanese prints - A way ahead; Gauguin, Van Gogh and the Post Impressionists ("The cursed generation").

Within the scope of this book, the main French Impressionists have been covered. Paradoxically the theories of the movement soon came to be abruptly discarded just at that point when their pictures were beginning to sell. Their successors, Van Gogh, Cézanne and Gauguin were dissatisfied with the axiom that truth could be captured and conveyed at a glance and came to distrust the reverence for optical sensation alone. These three, each in their own way, sought to delve deeper into the mysterious processes of art. Cézanne tried to render the forms of nature through "pyramid, cylinder and cone". He wanted "to make of Impressionism something solid and durable, like the art of the museums, to carve out the underlying structure of things". Van Gogh saw the Impressionists' work when he first came to Paris in 1886 and it helped to lift him out of the acute frustration and despair he was feeling at the time he arrived in the city at the age of 33. A new vivacity and brightness settled onto his palette as his paintings in the Montmartre district show. Gauguin, on the other hand was influenced by Impressionist art when he decided to make the most monumental decision in his life – to leave his wife and children after twelve years of marriage and his career as a stockbroker to become a full time painter. His point of departure came when he went painting in Pontoise with Pissarro, whom he stuck with for many years and exhibited with in the Impressionist exhibitions of 1880, 1882 and 1886. Gauguin was steeped in the work of the Impressionists (he amassed a huge collection of their paintings) and learnt his compositional skills from Manet whose *Olympia* he copied in 1891. Gauguin was to go on and carry forward the lessons he learnt from Impressionism: chiefly the love of sunshine and bright colour, a freedom of composition and the influence of Japanese art. All these he brought to his well-known Tahitian paintings of the 1890's, but it was earlier, with his move to Pont-Aven in Brittany in the summer of 1886 that he first put behind him the Impressionist credo of fidelity to immediate sensation alone.

He started striving towards a non-naturalistic and symbolic art which delved deep into the psyche and the primitive unconscious. Once in Tahiti he married the flat heraldic patterns of Japanese art to the climatic brilliance and exoticism of the native women to produce paintings rich in metaphor and symbol, paintings made

Paul Cézanne
drawing by Camille Pissarro

Selfportrait by Paul Gauguin

superficially so accessible to us now through their decorative immediacy. In fact the complexity of Gauguin's private symbolism has still not been fully revealed. Gauguin, like Cézanne, set out to analyse, and question the assumptions of their mentors, the Impressionists and to probe the deep underlying truths of fantasy and metaphor – to tear away the patchwork eiderdown of colour that the Impressionists had thrown over objects. Once the top blankets were off, the bed-frame stood revealed. Both Gauguin and Cézanne, like Lazarus, were prepared to pick up their beds and walk, making themselves both martyrs and outcasts in the process.

A way ahead

Impressionism is the true precursor of 20th century art. Its deliberately breaking down of forms and its exercises in colour abstraction anticipate Mondrian and Mark Rothko. Both Monet, in his water-lily studies at Giverny and Turner, in his swirling harbour mists say things that much recent abstract art when preoccupied with atmosphere and texture has not managed to add to or surpass.

Out of the movement were born the four great geniuses whose achievements straddled the last century and this – Cézanne, Van Gogh, Gauguin and Toulouse-Lautrec – whose work in their later years was termed "Post Impressionist". The battles the Impressionists fought in their time were the major battles of modern art – to break through the prejudices and assumptions of "socially accepted art". In the last three decades of the 19th century, European conciousness and sensibility was radically changed. We see the results of this all around us now. It led to the defiance of the modern artist to accept his work on his terms, his refusal to be hemmed in by the medium or environment and a steadfast opposition to establishment values. All these stances are the direct consequences of the courageous questioning and unswerving initiative shown by the Impressionists in their day.

But what we treasure above all are the marvellous, light soaked shimmering visions of landscape that shine out at us from gallery walls all around the world and never seem to dim in their brilliance and "joie de vivre". These are what make Impressionist works the most eternally popular and best loved paintings of all time.

Bibliography

The author has consulted the following works in the writing of this book:

The History of Impressionism
by John Rewald

The Lost World of the Impressionists
by Alice Bellony-Rewald
Modern Franch Painters
by R.H. Wilenski
Painters of Light; the Impressionists
by Keith Roberts
Monet at Giverny
by Claire Joyes
Impressionism, preface
by René Huyghe

The World of the Impressionists
by François Mathey
The Impressionists
by Denis Thomas
Renoir, my Father
by Jean Renoir
The Shock of the New
by Ian Dunlop.